PEOPLES OF THE ANCIENT WORLD

Life in the Ancient Indus River Valley

Westfield Middle School
Media Center

Hazel Richardson

Crabtree Publishing Company
www.crabtreebooks.com

Crabtree Publishing Company
www.crabtreebooks.com

For Eben, Oliver, and Thomas

Coordinating editor: Ellen Rodger

Editors: Rachel Eagen, Carrie Gleason, Adrianna Morganelli

Production coordinator: Rosie Gowsell

Production assistance: Samara Parent

Art director: Rob MacGregor

Project Management

International Book Productions, Inc.

Barbara Hopkinson

Judy Phillips

J. David Ellis

Dietmar Kokemohr

Sheila Hall

Consultant: Karl Schmidt, PhD., Associate Professor of History, South Dakota State University and Editor-in-Chief, Project South Asia

Photographs: India Unveiled by Robert Arnett: p. 24 (right); Associated Press, AP: p. 21 (bottom); Courtesy Australian Woodcrafts: p. 30 (top); Christie's Images/ CORBIS: p. 3; Courtesy Dharmakshetra: p. 18 (bottom); DK Images: p. 7; Greg Elms/ Lonely Planet Images: p. 19 (top); George Georgiou/ Panos Pictures: p. 31(bottom); Harappa Archaeological Research Project, Courtesy Dept. of Archaeology and Museums, Govt. of Pakistan: p. 22 (all); Harappa.com: pp. 4-5, p. 11 (top); Lindsey Hebberd/ CORBIS: p. 21 (top); Angelo Hornak/ CORBIS: p. 19 (bottom), p. 25 (right); Courtesy Islami city: p. 27 (top); Jeff Jonas: p. 16 (bottom); J.M. Kenoyer, Courtesy Sept. of Archaeology and Museums Govt. of Pakistan: p. 8, p. 9 (bottom), p. 11 (bottom), p. 16 (top), p. 22, p. 30 (bottom); Dave King/ DK Images: p. 9 (top); Diego Lezama Orezzoli/ CORBIS: p. 28; Courtesy Pfizer Inc: p. 27 (bottom); Reuters/ Punit Paranjpe: p. 25 (left); Scala/ Art Resource, NY: p. 24 (left); Photo Karl J. Schmidt: p. 20; Cecil Treal and Jean Michel Ruiz/ DK Images: p. 26; Brian A. Vikander/ CORBIS: p. 31 (top); Bill Wassman/ Lonely Planet Images: p. 17

Illustrations: William Band: borders, pp. 4–5 (timeline), p. 7 (bottom), p. 10, p. 11 (coin), pp. 12–13, p. 14, p. 15 (bottom), p. 23, p. 28 (top), p. 29

Cover: A priest or king figure excavated from the ancient Harappan city of Mohenjo-daro, located in what is now southern Pakistan, on the bank of the Indus River.

Contents: *Rajas*, or kings, continued to rule well past ancient times, as shown in this painting from the 1500s.

Title page: A detail from an illustrated reconstruction of a Harappan city shows farmers working outside the massive walls of the city.

Crabtree Publishing Company

www.crabtreebooks.com   1–800–387–7650

Cataloging-in-Publication Data
Richardson, Hazel.
  Life in the ancient Indus River Valley / written by Hazel Richardson.
     p. cm. -- (Peoples of the ancient world)
  Includes index.
  ISBN-13: 978-0-7787-2040-9 (rlb)
  ISBN-10: 0-7787-2040-3 (rlb)
  ISBN-13: 978-0-7787-2070-6 (pbk)
  ISBN-10: 0-7787-2070-5 (pbk)
  1. Indus River Valley--Civilization--Juvenile literature. I. Title. II.
Series.
  DS425.R53 2005
  934--dc22
                                        2005001097
                                           LC

Published in the United States
PMB 16A
350 Fifth Ave.
Suite 3308
New York, NY
10118

Published in Canada
616 Welland Ave.
St. Catharines
Ontario, Canada
L2M 5V6

Published in the United Kingdom
73 Lime Walk
Headington
Oxford
OX3 7AD
United Kingdom

Published in Australia
386 Mt. Alexander Rd.
Ascot Vale (Melbourne)
V1C 3032

Contents

Indus Civilization

Two of the world's greatest ancient civilizations began in the Indus River Valley, in what is now Pakistan. The earliest was the Harappans, who built highly advanced cities from 2600 B.C. to 1900 B.C. In 1750 B.C., the Aryans, a warrior people from the north, invaded the Indus River Valley and then spread across ancient India.

The Harappans

The Harappans were a wealthy nation of farmers, **craftspeople**, and traders. Five thousand years ago, the Harappans built clay-walled cities that had sewage systems for carrying water into and out of homes. They were also one of the first peoples to build sailing ships. The Harappans developed a system of writing to record their trade and their lives that scholars cannot understand today.

▶ *The ruins of the ancient city of Harappa were excavated in 1922. Harappa was built in 3600 B.C., and the Harappan civilization was named after it.*

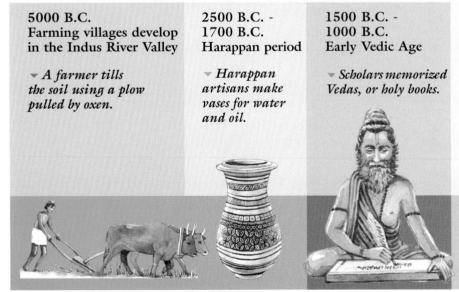

5000 B.C. Farming villages develop in the Indus River Valley	2500 B.C. - 1700 B.C. Harappan period	1500 B.C. - 1000 B.C. Early Vedic Age	1000 B.C. - 500 B.C. Late Vedic Age	560 B.C. - 480 B.C.
▾ *A farmer tills the soil using a plow pulled by oxen.*	▾ *Harappan artisans make vases for water and oil.*	▾ *Scholars memorized Vedas, or holy books.*	▾ *Indian silver bar coins are made and used from around 590 B.C.*	▾ *Siddhartha Gautama, the Buddha, travels and spreads beliefs.*

The Aryans Arrive

The Aryans were **nomadic** peoples who lived in what is now **central Asia**. When the Aryans moved into the Indus River Valley, historians think they intermixed with the Harappans. Over time, the Aryan culture spread from the Indus further south into the Ganges River Valley, creating the ancient Indian civilization. Historians once believed that the Aryans destroyed the Harappans, who are also called the ancient Indus River Valley civilization, but there is no **archaeological** evidence of this.

What is a "civilization?"

Most historians agree that a civilization is a group of people that shares common languages, some form of writing, advanced technology and science, and systems of government and religion.

327 B.C.

▼ *Alexander the Great marches into India.*

321 B.C. - 185 B.C.
Mauryan Age

▼ *Elephants are used in battles.*

273 B.C. - 232 B.C.
Rule of Asoka

Great temples are built.

320 A.D. - 540 A.D.
Gupta Age

▶ *Indian belief system has Ganges River as a goddess.*

A Land of Riches

The Indus River is one of the world's longest rivers. It starts in Tibet, in the Himalaya Mountains, and empties into the Arabian Sea in present-day Pakistan. The area where it empties is called the Indus River Valley.

The Lifeblood of the Valley

Today, the Indus River Valley is a dry, barren area, but thousands of years ago, it was lush. Each spring, melting ice and snow from the Himalaya Mountains rushed down streams and into the Indus and Saraswati rivers. Heavy summer **monsoon** rains also brought a lot of water, which caused the rivers to overflow. Muddy water, or silt, from the bursting rivers covered the surrounding **floodplains**, keeping the soil **fertile**.

The Bountiful Earth

Harappan farmers grew barley, wheat, melons, and dates. These crops were used to feed a growing population. They also grew cotton, which they used to make cloth for clothing. Surplus, or extra, crops were loaded onto sailboats to trade with Mesopotamia, or modern-day Iraq. The Harappans also herded sheep, goats, and a type of cattle called zebus on nearby pastures, and caught fish in the Arabian Sea.

▶ *Around 1800 B.C., the Indus River changed its course, moving slightly eastward. At the same time, another ancient river, the Saraswati, or Ghaggar-Hakra, dried up and disappeared. The Ganges River, holy to the ancient Indians, runs from the Himalayas to the Bay of Bengal.*

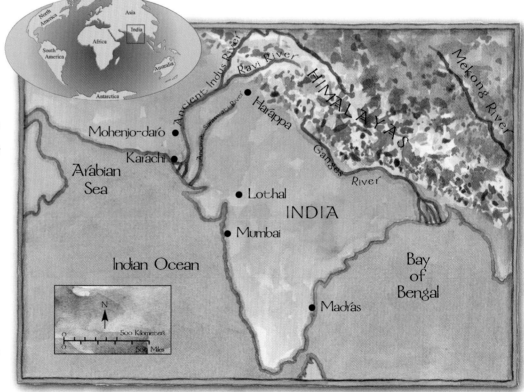

Metals and Minerals

The Himalaya Mountains in the north were a source of **flint**, which the Harappans made into blades and other tools. Copper and tin were mined and used to make saws, axes, and chisels. Forests to the west provided wood for tool handles, as well as firewood. Even the plains of the Thar Desert to the east were a resource. The Harappans used gemstones found there, such as **lapis lazuli** and turquoise, in jewelry they traded with other peoples.

▶ *A stream created from melting glaciers in the mountains of Tibet runs into the Indus River.*

Fighting the Floods

The Harappans' cities were destroyed many times by floodwaters from the Indus River. There were no stones nearby to make flood walls, so the Harappans built defense walls around their cities made out of clay bricks. The bricks were baked in a large oven, called a kiln, to harden them.

▶ *The Harappan flood defense walls were about 5 feet (1.5 meters) wide.*

Disaster Strikes

Historians believe that the
Harappan civilization may have
ended because of environmental
changes. By 1800 B.C., the people had destroyed most of
the forests around the valley because they used the wood to
fuel their ovens. At about the same time, the Saraswati River,
also known as the Ghaggar-Hakra River, dried up and the
Indus River changed its course, possibly because of an
earthquake. Very little rain falls in the Indus River Valley
between the annual monsoons, and when the floodwaters
from the rivers were lost, the surrounding farmland dried up.
In other places, the shift in the Indus River's course meant
towns built along the riverbanks were no longer on the banks
and therefore lost the income they received from trade. The
shift also caused devastating floods.

▲ *The dusty remains of the*
Harappan city of Mohenjo-daro.
Archaeologists found skeletons lying
where people had fallen in the
streets. Historians do not know if the
Harappans were killed by floods,
disease, or migrating Aryan peoples.

▲ *Harappan pottery was made from*
clay found near the riverbanks.

Eastward to the Ganges River Valley

Beginning in 1750 B.C. and for the next 200 to 300 years, huge waves of Aryans poured into the Indus Valley from the north on camels and horses. Some Aryans settled there to farm and trade as the Harappans had with neighboring **nations** around the Arabian Sea and Persian Gulf. Other Aryans traveled east over the desert to reach the Ganges River Valley. The Aryans spent hundreds of years clearing the thick jungles found on the plains alongside the Ganges River to make the land suitable for farming. Rice became a major crop, along with several types of millet, a grass grown for its grain.

▼ The Ganges River Valley was packed with dense jungles where thousands of elephants and tigers roamed freely. Today, India has the largest tiger population in the world.

▼ A Harappan carving shows a cage of compass birds onboard a trading ship. The Harappans traveled great distances to trade with Mesopotamians. Sailors had no compasses at the time, so they used the position of the stars to navigate at night. By day, they used birds called compass birds. When sailors lost sight of the coast, they released the birds, which flew toward land.

A Trading Nation

The ancient Indus River Valley was a paradise for traders. By 2000 B.C., the Harappans were trading grain, cloth, and gems from China to Persia, or present-day Iran. Following in the Harappans' footsteps, the Aryans exchanged goods to the same peoples on the same routes.

Overland Trade

Traders used pack animals, including two-humped camels, elephants, and carts pulled by bulls to carry goods overland. They traveled long distances over mountain routes through Afghanistan, Persia, and eastern China.

Valuable Goods

The Harappans exchanged grain, copper pots and pans, mirrors, elephant ivory, cotton cloth, lapis lazuli, shells, and **ceramic** jewelry for silver from Persia and Afghanistan, and gold and dried fish from Mesopotamia.

Sea Trade

Harappan boats laden with goods sailed up the **Persian Gulf** toward Persia and Mesopotamia. These month-long voyages were timed to take advantage of monsoon winds. Ships left Harappan ports between November and April, when the winds blew northeast. They returned between July and September, when winds blew southwest.

▲ *Caravans of elephants carried goods along trade routes. All the major Harappan towns and cities were along these routes. Later, the routes were used by Aryan traders as well.*

◀ *The enormous dockyard at the ancient Harappan city of Lothal. The docks were joined to the sea by a long canal where Harappans loaded ships with trade goods before sailing to Persia and Mesopotamia.*

Money, Money, Money

For thousands of years, the people of the Indus River Valley and ancient India used a barter, or swapping, system, rather than money. Silver bar coins were first used in ancient India long after the Aryans were established. The coins came to India from Persia, and were bar-shaped with symbols.

Exchanging Ideas

As they traded with other nations, the Harappans learned new skills. The Harappans learned how to make simple plows, called *ards*, from the Mesopotamians. Later, the ancient Indians began growing rice brought by Chinese traders. Rice then became a main crop of farmers.

▶ *Neither the Harappans nor the Aryans had coins for trading. When the silver bar coin was first used in ancient India, it made it easier to trade because all items had a standard value.*

An Ancient Unicorn

All Harappan trade goods had a pottery seal attached to them. Seals had writing and an image of an animal on them. Sometimes the animal was an elephant, a rhinoceros, or a bull, which represented gods. A unicorn was the most common image on seals. Some historians think that the unicorn was the symbol of the Harappan people or government. Around 1900 B.C., when the Harappan civilization started to decline, the unicorn image was no longer made on seals.

▲ *A Harappan unicorn seal.*

Cities Made of Clay

Ancient Harappan cities were built from baked clay bricks and had citadels **on raised clay blocks at the center. The two greatest Harappan cities were Harappa and Mohenjo-daro. Up to 50,000 people lived in Harappa, and 30,000 in Mohenjo-daro.**

1. Thick walls kept Indus floodwaters away from the city. After the waters receded, the fertile soil made for excellent farmland.

2. Every city had granaries for storing food, factories for making beads, and kilns for baking bricks.

3. The Harappans were concerned with bathing and cleanliness and even included bathing as part of their religious ceremonies. Every household had access to a water well, and nearly all houses had a bathroom.

4. The Harappans had indoor plumbing and sewage systems thousands of years before most other civilizations. Clay drainpipes ran from the houses to larger, covered drainways on the streets that carried sewage and wastewater out of the city.

5. Houses were one or two stories high, with flat roofs. People slept outside on the roofs on hot summer nights. Exterior walls had no windows. Small windows opened onto a central courtyard and kept rooms cool.

6. Merchants sold goods from shops and stalls in city streets.

7. Seals were pressed onto clay tabs and the tabs were attached to goods going to market.

Life of the Aryans

The Aryans' holy books, called the Vedas, are a historical record of their lives. Many stories in the Vedas tell of chariot battles between Aryans, and against other peoples of the Indus and Ganges River Valleys.

Tribal Life

The Aryans lived in *ganas*, which means "collections." A *gana* was made up of several families. Each *gana* had its own territory, ruled by a warrior chief called a *raja*, or king. Most *gana* houses were small and built of wood and straw and had only one room, where all family members lived. Historians believe that the families of rulers and **nobles** lived in larger homes.

Fireside Tales

Aryan homes had a central **hearth**, called the *yagna*. Family members gathered around the *yagna* to eat and share news of the day. Food was cooked over the fire using roasting spits and bronze cauldrons. The Aryans ate fruit, vegetables, wheat, barley, rice, beef, goat, and **mutton.** They also made butter from cow milk and drank cow and goat milk. The fire tender of the household had the important task of keeping the *yagna's* fire going. Fire was considered a gift from Agni, the fire god.

Did Aryans Destroy Harappan Cities?

The Rig-Veda is a collection of 1,000 hymns composed between 1500 B.C. and 800 B.C. Some of these hymns describe Aryan warriors destroying large cities and killing the dark-skinned, curly haired people who lived there. Some archaeologists think these stories describe the Aryans attacking the Harappans. Others believe the stories are exaggerations.

▲ *Aryan warriors in a chariot.*

▶ *A brahman priest teaching his students.*

The Caste System

The Aryans in the Indus Valley belonged to castes, or social levels. People were born into castes and could not move up or down. Aryan priests were *brahmans*, the highest social level. Warriors and rulers were *kshatriyas*. Farmers were members of the *vaisyas* caste, and servants and laborers were *sudras*. The Aryans called the indigenous people of the Indus Valley *dasas*, or the untouchables. *Dasas* were considered the lowest level in society. All caste members had to eat food prepared by members of their own caste, work in caste-specific jobs, and marry within their caste. Those who married outside their caste could be killed.

Women and Children

Until about 500 B.C., Aryan women were allowed to own property. Some were even famous warriors. Over time, the *brahmans* became powerful and developed new ideas, including the idea that women should be strictly controlled. A woman was not allowed to own property and had a husband chosen for her by her parents. Women were taught to obey male members of their family.

Most Aryan children began working at a young age. Farmers' sons herded animals, while daughters did housework and fetched water. Boys of the *brahman* caste went to school to learn the sacred Vedas from *gurus*. Boys from wealthy families were taught mathematics and astronomy, but girls had no formal education.

◀ *An Aryan man placed a spot of his blood on his bride's forehead as a sign that she belonged to him.*

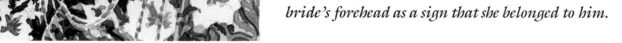

Rulers and Empires

Historians are still learning about Harappan government. They know each city had a ruler, who lived in a central palace. Historians believe that the ruler and his advisors formed a government that determined how a city was built because all Harappan cities were built in the same way.

Aryan Kingdoms

By 600 B.C., most Aryans had settled by the Ganges River Valley. This area was divided into sixteen kingdoms, each ruled by a *raja*. The most powerful kingdom was Magadha.

The Mauryan Age

In 321 B.C., a *raja* named Chandragupta Maurya killed the *raja* of Magadha and made himself emperor. Chandragupta Maurya was not afraid to kill those who went against his ideas. By the end of his reign, Chandragupta Maurya's territory extended from the Ganges and Indus rivers to most of Afghanistan. The capital of his empire, Pataliputra, had elaborate temples, a university, a library, and public parks. Chandragupta Maurya and the emperors who followed him established a period of rule called the Mauryan Empire.

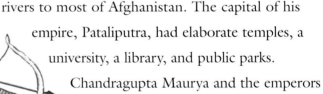

▲ *A priest or king figure excavated from the ancient Harappan city of Mohenjo-daro, on the bank of the Indus River.*

◁ *Elephants were used in battle by many dynasties in ancient India.*

The Reign of Asoka

Chandragupta's grandson, Asoka, was one of India's most famous rulers. In 260 B.C., Asoka sent his army to conquer the native peoples of southern India. The slaughter that followed horrified Asoka. He began to study the new Indian religion of Buddhism, which said killing is wrong and that all men are equal and deserve respect. He was so impressed with Buddhist ideas that he made Buddhism the official religion of his kingdom. Asoka ordered thousands of stone pillars and stupas, or monuments whose domed shape is said to represent the Buddha, to be raised across India. The stupas were carved to show laws on how to behave. These laws were known as *dharma*.

End of an Empire

When the ruler of the Mauryans was **assassinated** in 185 B.C., the empire broke apart. For 500 years, India was again divided into smaller, separate kingdoms. In 320 A.D., a minor **chieftain** named Chandra Gupta took power and became the emperor. The empire he set up was expanded by the rulers who came after him until it came to include the entire north of India, from the Bay of Bengal to the Arabian Sea. This empire united the north of India for 220 years.

▼ *A stupa with a carved pillar gateway. Asoka commanded that there be respect for the dignity of all men, religious tolerance, and non-violence.*

Religions and Beliefs

Archaeologists think the Harappans worshipped many gods. When the Aryans invaded the Indus River Valley, they brought their religion with them. Over the next 1,000 years, the Aryans' religion changed, borrowing beliefs from Harappan and other cultures. Over time, Aryan beliefs developed into the Hindu religion. Other religions also developed in ancient India.

Harappan Beliefs

It is hard to know exactly what the Harappans believed because nobody can understand their form of writing, or **script**. Archaeologists think they worshipped many human and animal gods, as well as tree and river spirits. They also believed in some form of life after death. Harappans put pottery jars in the graves of their dead. The jars contained food to be eaten in the afterlife.

▲ *Harappans buried their dead in pits, with the bodies laid out in coffins in a north-south direction, often with tools or simple jewelry.*

▶ *The Aryans believed that each year Varuna, god of the heavens, fought an enormous dragon. The monsoon rains came only if Varuna defeated the dragon.*

Aryan Gods

The Aryans believed that gods, or *devas*, controlled all things in nature, such as weather, fire, and water. They also believed that helper gods created wealth and happiness, healed illnesses, protected roads, and even got people out of bed each morning. One such god was Shiva, Lord of Creatures. Shiva may also have been a Harappan god.

Burning the Dead

One of the most important Aryan gods was Agni, the god of fire. Aryans cremated, or burned, their dead, in the belief that Agni carried the souls to heaven. Even though Hindus today do not believe in an afterlife, they continue to cremate their dead.

Reincarnation

The early Aryans believed in an afterlife. Good people went to heaven, while evil people were cast into a pit of blackness. The pit was replaced by a belief in reincarnation, or that every living thing goes through a series of lives.

▼ *Kali, the Hindu goddess of death, is often shown drinking blood or wearing a skull.*

Karma

Hindus believe people are reborn, or reincarnated, after they die. What they are reincarnated as depends on karma, which in turn depends on how that person acted in previous lives. Someone who does good deeds builds up good karma. In the new life, that person may be wealthier or in a higher caste than in the previous life. A person with bad karma is reborn into a low caste, as an animal, or even as a plant. Hindu *brahmans* used the law of karma to explain the caste system. They believed that a person was born a *dasa* because that person had been bad in a previous life.

▲ *Funeral pyres line the sacred Ganges River in India's most holy city of Varanasi. Like their ancient ancestors, Hindus cremate, or burn, their dead.*

Ending the Cycle

The cycle of reincarnation ends only when a person becomes aware of being one with the universe upon death. Release from the cycle can be achieved by devout worship of one of the many Hindu gods.

The Buddha

In 560 B.C., Siddhartha Gautama was born into a wealthy Hindu family. When he was 29 years old, he became aware of suffering, and set out in search of an answer to human misery. For six years, Siddhartha wandered across India, visiting great teachers, or *gurus*. Then, at the age of 35, he spent a night under a tree in meditation. He had visions of his former lives and suddenly understood the cause of misery and cycle of reincarnation.

Nirvana

In Siddhartha Gautama's awakening, or enlightenment, he saw no suffering, greed, or hatred. He called this nirvana, and believed it was something a person could reach by following a set of eight rules for living which he called the eightfold path. His followers called him the Buddha, or Enlightened One. Buddhism was spread throughout India and the rest of Asia by traveling monks and holy men. Many people adopted the religion because they felt it helped relieve their suffering. The Buddha's teachings developed into a religion that still exists today, 2,500 years after the Buddha was born.

▼ *Buddhists do not believe in gods. Their holy statues are of the Buddha. Farmlands in the Indus River Valley are still home to many ancient Buddha statues, even in places where the people no longer follow the ancient religion.*

Jainism

Jainism is a religion based on the idea that people should be truthful, not want too much, and not steal or use violence against other living things. Jains follow the teachings of Vardhamana Mahavira, who lived at the same time as Buddha. Mahavira was a prince who gave up his wealth and traveled around India, **meditating** and teaching. One of his most important teachings was to not harm other living things, including animals and plants. Today, nearly four million Jains still follow this ancient religion.

▶ *Very religious Jains wear masks over their mouths so they will not breathe in and kill insects.*

▼ *Zoroastrianism is an ancient religion that began in Persia, or present-day Iran 3,500 years ago. Followers of this religion in India are called Parsis. The Parsis migrated from Persia around 900 A.D. They built temples, which they call fire temples, and they believe fire is sacred.*

Words and Writing

The Harappans developed a system of writing which they used to record events and trade they did with other peoples. The Aryans' Sanskrit language is still used today in religious ceremonies.

Harappan Symbols

Harappan writing has been found on many pieces of pottery and stone. Some of it dates from 3500 B.C., which means that the Harappans were one of the first civilizations to use writing. Like other ancient civilizations, such as the Egyptians, early Harappan writing was based on pictographs which made up a type of alphabet.

Harappan writing is a mystery to people today. No more than 20 symbols were ever carved on a tablet or seal. Nobody knows why or has been able to decipher the script. Researchers think that each symbol stands for a syllable rather than a letter and that the language was similar to Dravidian, a language still spoken by peoples in southern India.

▲ *Harappan seals had a carved inscription on top of a depiction of a scene or animal.*

◄ *The Harappans had about 300 symbols which were simplified to make carving easier. Symbols ran from left to right on the top line, and then from right to left on the next.*

An Ancient Tongue

The Aryans brought two languages with them when they came to the Indus Valley in about 1500 B.C. The first was Dardic, which has since disappeared. The second one was Sanskrit.

Sanskrit is called an Indo-European language because it developed in the area between Europe, India, and Asia. It is similar to the European languages Latin, used in ancient Rome, and ancient Greek. The Sanskrit word for mother is "matr," and the word for father is "pitr." In Latin, these words are "mater" and "pater."

Today, Sanskrit is used only by *brahmans*, the Hindu priests, to read and write religious books, but some Sanskrit words are found in many modern languages, including Thai.

Written Sanskrit

The ancient Indians did not develop a written system of Sanskrit for more than 1,000 years. Their holy books, the Vedas, were memorized and passed down from *brahman* to *brahman*. The first known Sanskrit writing is a copy of the Rig Veda holy book written around 400 B.C.

▼ *An ancient scholar works on a Veda, or holy book, written in Sanskrit.*

Sacred Books

The Vedas are a collection of hymns, stories, and rituals of the ancient Indians. They are a record of what life was like 4,000 years ago in India. The four Veda books, the Rig Veda, Sama Veda, Yajur Veda, and the Atharva Veda are studied by religious scholars, historians and linguists, or people who study and compare languages. There are many other ancient Indian books. The Mahabharata and the Ramayana are thought to be the longest poems in any language and each take up several books. The Mahabharata is the legend of a group of Aryans called the Bharatas. The Ramayana is a love poem.

Arts and Culture

The Harappans were skilled artists and musicians. The ancient Indians were accomplished stone carvers who erected beautiful temples. Their exciting myths and founding stories are some of the greatest tales ever written.

Magnificent Temples

The greatest artworks of ancient Indian civilization are its temples. By 400 B.C., Indians were skilled stoneworkers, having learned from the ancient Greeks, with whom they traded. From 320 A.D. to 540 A.D., beautiful stone temples with magnificent carvings were built all over northern India.

Harappan Art

Music, beauty, and art were important to the Harappans. They invented stringed musical instruments that looked like harps, and filled their towns and cities with beautiful statues, carved pottery, and furniture inlaid with precious stones.

▲ *The carvings on Hindu temples such as this one depict scenes from the Vedas.*

◄ *This statue of a dancing girl is the most famous piece of Harappan art. Music and dancing were important parts of Harappan life.*

 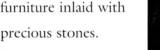

▲ *Festivals honoring Ganesh's birth are still celebrated in modern India.*

Hindu Literature

The ancient Indians wrote the world's longest story. It is called the Mahabharata, and was written in about 200 A.D. The most famous part of it is called the Bhagavad-Gita, or Song of the Lord. It is a very long poem about a warrior who talks to a god called Lord Krishna, who is disguised as a chariot driver.

India's greatest poet and playwright, Kalidasa, lived sometime between 450 A.D. and the early 500s A.D. Little is known about his life. A follower of the goddess Kali, Kalidasa is said to have prayed to the goddess, who rewarded him with his great gift for words. Kalidasa wrote long poems in Sanskrit. The plays he wrote, all of which have happy endings, were the first known plays performed in India.

Ancient Indian Festivals

Ancient Indians had more festivals and holy days than any other civilization. People fasted, bathed, chanted, drank, and offered gifts to *brahmans*. One festival celebrated the birthday of Ganesh, the elephant-headed god of luck, believed to have been born while his mother, the love goddess, Parvati, was having a bath. Worshippers at Ganesh festivals broke open coconuts in front of clay figures of Ganesh to show they destroyed their pride.

Rama and Hanuman

One famous piece of Indian literature is the Ramayana, written in 200 A.D. It is the story of Prince Rama, who is sent to a forest for fourteen years by a rival half-brother and his jealous mother. While Rama is away, his wife, Sita, is kidnapped by a wicked demon. Rama finds her with the help of his friend, Hanuman, the monkey.

▲ *Scene from the Ramayana.*

Amazing Inventions

The Harappans developed building techniques that helped them to defend their cities against floods and bring water to their fields, or irrigate. As skilled metalworkers, they also invented tools such as drills and needles.

Master Builders

The Harappans dug wells 100 feet (30 meters) deep to provide their cities with water. They also built underground drains to take waste out of the city using stone and bronze tools. Bricks and roads were made **standard**, and buildings were constructed using precise measurements. Their smallest unit of measure was 0.06 inches (1.5 mm). No other civilization of the time could measure anything that small.

Enduring Technologies

Many technologies used around the world today were first used by the Harappans. Bronze tools used in building, including the circular saw and drill, were Harappan inventions. **Stoneware** pottery for dishes and storage jars was designed by Harappan craftspeople. The Harappans were also the first to weave and print on cotton cloth, which they used for clothing and for wrapping goods.

▼ *Harappan potters used a bowl to spin pottery, similar to how a pottery wheel works today.*

Great Mathematicians

The most amazing ancient Indian discoveries were in mathematics. Every student in the world uses some of these discoveries. In 497 A.D., the **mathematician** Aryabhata developed the **decimal system**, which simplified calculations. He also determined that the Earth orbits the Sun, something European astronomers did not realize until 1,000 years later. By 600 A.D., Indians had invented the numerical symbols that evolved into the numbers 1 to 9. They also may have developed the concept of zero.

▲ *Early and later Indian numerals are shown in the top two rows. The bottom two rows show their development into modern numbers.*

The Science of Life

Ancient Indian medicine emphasized cleanliness and disease prevention. India had hospitals and used herbs for medicine as early as 400 B.C. In 500 B.C., an Indian doctor named Susrata performed the first cataract operation on a patient's eyes. Doctors in ancient India were also skilled at plastic surgery. Cutting off the nose was a punishment for some crimes, and doctors found a way to rebuild the nose using skin from the cheek.

▲ *Sage Susrata was one of the world's first plastic surgeons in 500 B.C.*

From Rise to Ruin

By 1900 B.C., the Harappan civilization was in decline. Some cities and towns were abandoned. The Harappans disappeared between 1900 B.C. and 1700 B.C. and nobody knows exactly why. The Aryan civilization spread throughout India, adapting and changing over time. Many different peoples invaded India and left their mark.

Floods and Droughts

Archaeologists only began to study the great cities of the Harappan civilization in the 1920s. The work has been slow and there is no agreement yet on what exactly happened to the Harappans. The cities of Harappa and Mohenjo-daro are still being excavated but archaeologists know that they survived and were rebuilt after several ancient floods. Some archaeologists believe the Harappans left the cities to live in smaller groups after the Hakra River dried up and the Indus changed course. Others think the desert began to creep into the fertile farmlands. The changes to the environment around the Indus altered the economy of the area and may have made the civilization decline.

▲ *Alexander the Great was a Macedonian warrior who conquered the Indus River Valley in 327 B.C.*

▾ *The granaries of Mohenjo-daro. At its height, the Indus civilization spread over half a million square miles (130,000 square kilometers).*

Invasions and Conquerors

India's ancient history is one of invasion and adaptation. The Aryans were the first invaders to leave their mark. In 500 B.C., Aryan India was invaded by the Persians who conquered the Indus River Valley. The Persian rulers were then conquered by the Greeks in 327 B.C., led by Macedonian general, Alexander the Great. Alexander returned to Greece but left men behind to look after trade routes he established.

▼ This carved stone lion was originally on top of a Buddhist stupa in India. The image is now the national emblem of India.

Mauryan and Gupta Empires

After Alexander left, an Indian ruler named Chandragupta Maurya reconquered the Indus River Valley and parts of northern India. Chandragupta Maurya died in 298 B.C. His descendants continued the family rule known as the Mauryan empire. Over time, the Mauryan empire weakened and fell apart. India then split into a number of smaller kingdoms that were often invaded by other peoples such as the Greeks, and the Persians.

In 320 A.D., another strong ruler named Chandra Gupta brought India under his control. Chandra Gupta was not related to Chandragupta Maurya. His empire was called the Gupta empire. The Gupta empire spread south and over hundreds of years made great advances in art, science, and literature. The empire fell apart in 550 A.D. after the Huns, invaders from western China, took over parts of the empire.

Other Invaders

After the Gupta empire, India returned to being a nation of **city-states** ruled by kings, or *rajas*. In the south, the **indigenous** peoples, called the Dravidians, lived in kingdoms divided from the north by forests and mountains that were difficult for armies to cross. In 1000 A.D., Arabs conquered the city-states in the north. The Arabs brought their religion, **Islam**, and over time, Muslim rulers established new empires called the Delhi Sultanate and the Moghul dynasty. The Moghul dynasty ruled northern India from the 1500s until the early 1800s, expanding with each ruler. After 1858, India came under British **colonial** rule, and the south and north were once again united.

Ancient Legacies

The Harappans were all but forgotten until 100 years ago. Now, historians are piecing together a record of their achievements, including some of the greatest innovations of ancient times, technologies still used today. The Ancient Indians' scientific achievements contributed to one of the world's most enduring cultures.

Living History

Many small farming communities in India and Pakistan are located near the sites of ancient Harappan and Indian cities and villages. Farmers still use some of the technology developed thousands of years ago, including ox carts and pottery wheels. Ancient Indian gods are worshipped in shrines, and ancient stupas still dot the countryside.

Chess, invented by the Ancient Indians, is the most famous board game in the world. The Indians also invented playing cards.

Indians in many communities today use camels and flat-bottomed boats, as the ancient Indians did.

Cotton Clothing

The Harappans were the first people to weave the fluffy heads, or bolls of a cotton plant, into thread. They passed this knowledge on as they traded with the Mesopotamians and Persians, and it spread around the world. Today, cotton textiles and clothing are still made in modern Pakistan and India and are exported around the world.

▼ A director's hand frames actors on a Bollywood movie set. Many Bollywood movies re-enact scenes from ancient Indian myths or religious books. Almost all Bollywood movies also feature many musical and dance numbers. Many of the dancers were trained in classical Indian dance, which began thousands of years ago as temple dancing.

Yards of Tradition

The traditional Indian dress for women is a sari. Many peasant men in India wear a dhoti, a piece of cloth wrapped around the waist and between the legs. Both were worn in ancient India 4,000 years ago.

▲ The sari is a long piece of silk or cotton cloth draped around the body, and sometimes the head.

Movie Heroes

Thousands of movies are made each year in India. Many Indian movies recreate ancient Indian myths and legends, including hymns from the Vedas. The movies keep history alive and teach moviegoers about the culture of ancient India. Most Indian movies are made in modern Mumbai, formerly known as Bombay, India's Hollywood or Bollywood. The movies almost always feature singing and dancing adapted from ancient, or classical Indian dance, and stories of ancient battles.

Glossary

ancient India The Indian subcontinent, which today includes the countries of India and Pakistan

archaeological Belonging to the study of the past through the examination of buildings and artifacts

assassinate To murder for political reasons

cataract A clouding of the eye lens that obstructs sight

central Asia An area from the Caspian Sea to the border of China

ceramic A type of glazed pottery

chieftain The leader of a band or clan

citadel A fortress that commands a city

city-state An independent city, usually walled for defense, and the surrounding towns and villages that depend upon it for defense

colonial Describing something from the time when a country was ruled and settled by another country

craftspeople People who make things such as pottery or art

decimal system A number system based on units of ten

excavate To dig out from the ground

fertile Able to produce abundant crops, vegetation, or offspring

flint A hard type of quartz

floodplain Flat areas next to a river that frequently flood

hearth An open area surrounding a fire

hymns Religious songs of praise and glory

indigenous Native to an area

inscription Words or letters marked, often by carving, on a surface

Islam A religion that follows the teachings of the prophet Muhammad

lapis lazuli A blue colored semiprecious stone

mathematician A person who is skilled or learned in mathematics

meditate To quietly think, or contemplate

monsoon Winds that bring heavy rain to south Asia

mutton Sheep meat

nation A group of people organized under one government

navigate To follow a course on land or water

nobles Persons of high birth, or status in society

nomadic Moving from place to place

Persian Gulf A narrow arm of the Arabian Sea between the Arabian peninsula and present-day Iran

pyre A pile of material that burns easily

script Recorded language

standard A measure of comparison

stoneware A heavy type of pottery

Index

1 2 3 4 5 6 7 8 9 0 Printed in the U.S.A. 4 3 2 1 0 9 8 7 6 5